THE U.S. WASP:

Trailblazing Women Pilots of World War II

by Lisa M. Bolt Simons

CAPSTONE PRESS
a capstone imprint

Snap Books are published by Capstone Press,
1710 Roe Crest Drive, North Mankato, Minnesota 56003
www.mycapstone.com

Library of Congress Cataloging-in-Publication Data
Names: Simons, Lisa M. B., 1969- author.Title: The U.S. WASP : trailblazing women pilots of World War II / by Lisa M. Bolt Simons. Other titles: Trailblazing women pilots of World War I
Description: North Mankato, Minnesota : Capstone Press, [2018] | Series: Women and war | "Snap Books." | Includes bibliographical references and index. |
Audience: Grades 4-6. | Audience: Ages 8-14.
Identifiers: LCCN 2017015339| ISBN 9781515779377 (library binding) | ISBN 9781515779445 (pbk.) |
 ISBN 9781515779483 (ebook pdf)
Subjects: LCSH: Women Airforce Service Pilots (U.S.)—History—Juvenile literature. | United States. Army Air Forces. Air Transport Command. Ferrying Division—History—Juvenile literature. | Women air pilots—United States—History—20th century—Juvenile literature. | World War, 1939–1945—Participation, Female—Juvenile literature. | World War, 1939–1945—Aerial operations, American—Juvenile literature. | World War, 1939–1945—Transportation—United States—Juvenile literature. | United States. Army Air Forces—Transportation—Juvenile literature. | Airplanes—United States—Ferrying—History—20th century—Juvenile literature.
Classification: LCC D790.5 .S63 2018 | DDC 940.54/4973082—dc23

LC record available at https://lccn.loc.gov/2017015339

Editorial Credits
Megan Atwood, editor; Veronica Scott, designer; Jo Miller, media researcher

Photo Credits
AP Images, 11; Corel, cover (bottom left, middle left, top left); DoD News: courtesy photo, 22; Getty Images: Archive Photos/PhotoQuest, 13, Bettmann, 7 (left), 10, 19, Corbis Historical/George Rinhart, 8, The LIFE Picture Collection/ Peter Stackpole, 5, 18, 23; Newscom: akg-images, 7 (right), Rapport Syndication/The White House/Peter Souza, 25; Shutterstock: Everett Historical, 6, Everett Historical, cover (bottom right), Gary Blakeley, cover (top right), Rainer Lesniewski, 14; U.S. Air Force photo, 15; Wikimedia: Photo U.S. Mint, 27 (inset), U.S. Air Force photo, 16, 20, 21, U.S. Air Force photo illustration/John Turner, 4, U.S. Air Force Public Affairs/Pete Souza, 27, U.S. Army, 24, 9

Design Elements
Shutterstock: Allexxandar, Eky Studio, udra11

TABLE OF CONTENTS

Chapter 1

THE WORLD AT WAR AGAIN

Hazel Ah Ying Lee sat in the back seat of the Fairchild PT-19. The PT-19, a trainer plane for the Women Airforce Service Pilots, or WASP, had two seats and an open cockpit. Her flight instructor was in the front seat.

Lee's flight instructor enjoyed performing loops — flying upside down in the air. But he had a habit of demonstrating them without warning students first. That day, Lee didn't know her seat belt wasn't buckled correctly. The instructor flew his loop, and Lee fell out of the plane. Luckily, she was wearing her parachute. She landed safely in a field and walked back to the base, dragging her parachute behind her.

Hazel Ah Ying Lee

Lee was one of over 1,000 women who joined the WASP during World War II (1939 – 1945). They had no idea they'd fly so far into history.

Pilot from the Women's Flying Training Detachment in a PT-19 army trainer

"I always wanted to fly. Ever since I can remember. I was a young tyke. I made so many model airplanes that my mother got tired of seeing them around the house."

— WASP Florence "Shutsy" Reynolds

In World War I (1914 – 1918) almost 9 million people around the world died. The United States suffered more than 115,000 of those deaths. Only 20 years later, the world went to war again. Still recovering from their losses from the First World War, the United States needed more soldiers for combat. But women were not allowed to fight.

On December 7, 1941, Japan attacked Pearl Harbor in Hawaii. The Japanese used 353 airplanes for the invasion. Over 2,400 Americans died that day.

The bombing of Pearl Harbor

This event changed the role women played in the war. Suddenly, they were needed to fill jobs that traditionally belonged to men — those men were now needed to fight. But the United States government realized there weren't enough men to become pilots. Two female flyers, Jackie Cochran and Nancy Harkness Love, knew that women were capable pilots and could be invaluable in the war effort. Jackie and Nancy became responsible for helping women fly for their country.

Nancy Harkness Love

Jackie Cochran

Chapter 2

WOMEN WITH WINGS

The Harmon Trophy is given to outstanding aviators. Jackie won her first trophy after flying only four years. The next year, she won the trophy again and set new altitude and speed records.

After World War II began, Jackie sent a letter to U.S. first lady Eleanor Roosevelt. She wrote that women pilots could help the United States if it went to war. Although Roosevelt liked the idea, the military did not.

FACT

Jackie was the first woman to fly a bomber plane over the Atlantic Ocean on June 17, 1941.

Eleanor Roosevelt presents the Harmon Trophy to Jackie Cochran.

General Henry "Hap" Arnold

In 1941 Jackie ran into General Henry "Hap" Arnold, the chief of the Army Air Forces (AAF), at an event. She told him her idea about employing women as pilots. But Arnold wasn't ready for female pilots in the U.S. military. Later that year, Jackie asked him again. Arnold suggested she **ferry** planes in Britain, a country that already utilized female pilots. Jackie took his suggestion and employed 25 U.S. women in Britain. She hoped to prove they could someday fly for the U.S. military.

A Hard Worker

Jackie grew up poor, working in sawmills for six cents an hour. She became a beautician at age 13, and then later became a nurse. Saddened by poverty and disliking the sight of blood, she returned to working in beauty shops. In her 20s she told her future husband that she wanted to start a cosmetics company. He told her she needed to learn to fly to so she could get her products in more places around the country. It only took her a few weeks to get her private pilot's license. She became successful as both a pilot and businesswoman.

New WAFS members, dressed in flying suits and helmets, line up in front of their flight training facility.

Nancy Harkness was making history too. She earned her pilot's license when she was 16 years old — the youngest American woman to do so. After she married Bob Love and became Nancy Harkness Love, the two of them ran Inter City Aviation. The company gave flying classes and sold planes.

The shortage of male pilots on the front lines continued. Nancy flew airplanes from American factories to Canada. British pilots then flew the planes to England. Nancy approached the AAF in 1940 with an idea to ferry U.S. military planes. General Arnold rejected it, just as he had with Jackie's idea.

> "The myth of flying was 'a glamorous, long white scarf flying in the wind; the breeze in your face.' It was just that — a myth. The routine was back-breaking, hard, dirty work. It strained every ounce of endurance and courage we could muster."
>
> — *WASP Doris Tanner*

Two years later, the need for military pilots had grown urgent. Nancy met with a colonel, who took her idea to General Harold George, the Air Transport Command Commander. General George wrote about Nancy's idea to General Arnold, who finally approved it. The Women's Auxiliary Ferrying Squadron (WAFS) was established at New Castle AAF Base in Delaware. Nancy was commander. By December, 28 female pilots — the Originals — were sworn into civil service.

Nancy Harkness inspects the first group of WAFS pilots.

FACT

In college Nancy was grounded for "buzzing" — flying too close to campus — while showing off for friends. She was forced to go home for two weeks and couldn't fly for the rest of the semester.

Jackie Cochran found out about Nancy's ferrying program while she was in Britain. She was outraged. She'd been trying to start a women's pilot organization in the U.S. military since the war started.

Jackie returned to the United States and met with General Arnold. He directed General George and his assistant to solve the problem. They established the Women's Flying Training Detachment (WFTD) as part of the AAF to satisfy Jackie. She would train qualified women as pilots, who would then serve in Nancy's ferrying squadron.

FACT

The WASP program was created before the civil rights movement. Two Mexican-American women, two Chinese-American women, and one Native-American woman from the Oglala Lakota tribe became WASP. However, one African-American woman applicant withdrew after having lunch with Jackie. Jackie told her that she wanted to avoid any racial bias in the program. She felt it was already difficult enough to fight gender bias in the military. Consequently, the WASP program lost out on many good potential recruits because of racism.

Jackie Cochran (center) talks to a group of trainees.

Jackie's goal was to train 500 women the first year. Applications were sent to women across the nation. Around 30 of those who qualified became the first class on November 16, 1942, in Houston. The training program was 23 weeks long. Unlike the publicity Nancy's WAFS program received, recruits in the WFTD were told it was top secret. These women were the first to be trained as AAF pilots.

As 1943 began, Jackie moved her training program to Avenger Field in Sweetwater, Texas. The space was better for training. The military wanted 750 pilots by the end of 1943 and 1,000 in 1944. The first class started in February 1943.

Avenger Field

"I am enclosing a picture of our AT-6. This is real FLYING. The future of this experiment depends wholly on us. What a responsibility. Oh, there is never a dull day at Avenger."

— WASP Adaline Alma Blank in a letter to her sister

FACT

Avenger Field was the only training school in the AAF where students graduated at the same base where they started.

Dedicated to Serving

To qualify to train, women had to take and pay for their own flying lessons. Some women had to be creative to finance these lessons. Elizabeth "Betty" Wall (later known as Liz Strohfus) once heard someone talk about flying. "I thought, 'What a wonderful thing to get above it all and see the beautiful world there,'" she said. In order to join the local flying club in Faribault, Minnesota, for $100, Wall used her bike as collateral for the loan. She was a WASP in 1943 and 1944.

On July 5, 1943, General Arnold named Jackie the Director of Women Pilots, which she'd wanted all along. The same day, Nancy became the executive of the WAFS by Brigadier General Tunner. Jackie, however, still wanted to be the sole commander of one program, much to Nancy's displeasure.

In August 1943, General Arnold ordered the merging of the training and flying programs into the Women Airforce Service Pilots, or WASP, to include all the female pilots. Jackie continued as the director of the program in Washington, D.C. She was in charge of every phase, including recruitment, training, and assignments. Nancy's title became the Executive for the WASP/Ferrying Division, which kept her as commander of the ferrying pilots.

The training place of WASP

AVIATION ENTERPRISES LTD.

WASP TRAINING AND ASSIGNMENTS

More than 25,000 women across the United States applied for the WASP program. Jackie chose 1,830 women to report to Avenger Field. Of those, 552 didn't have the flying skills. Others quit, left for medical reasons, or got into trouble.

The trainees followed a schedule. It included three parts: military training, ground school, and flight training.

FACT

When the program first started, new arrivals had to take a swimming test. To pass, they had to swim from one end of Sweetwater's community pool to the other . . . in the uniform they wore to fly the planes.

WASP trainees with an instructor

WASP Applicant Qualifications

- between the ages of 21 and 35, later lowered to 18
- high school graduate
- minimum height of 60 inches (152 cm), later changed to 64 inches (163 cm)
- 200 flying hours, later changed to 35 hours
- have uncorrected 20/20 vision
- examined by an Army flight surgeon
- American citizen
- interviewed by a recruiting officer
- passed the written Aviation Cadet Qualifying Examination
- exceptions were made with age and height

Military training included drills, inspections, and organization. It also included training on chemical warfare, keeping military information classified, and participating in Army protocol and ceremonies.

Ground school included flight basics, reading maps and charts, and weather. Trainees also studied engines and propellers. Physics and math classes were required, as was first-aid training and Morse code.

In flight training, lighter training planes were used. Pilots also learned how to fly heavier, faster airplanes. Gradually, the focus switched to cross-country flights.

Trainees doing daily calisthenics

Once a pilot graduated, she earned a commercial pilot's license and an instrument rating. The rating meant that a pilot could fly when there was low visibility, such as in bad weather. Graduates also earned what was the same as a college aeronautical degree.

The WASP program had 1,074 graduates. With the addition of the "Originals" from Nancy's initial ferrying squadron, 1,102 pilots were ready to serve.

Pilots stayed at Sweetwater for duty or were assigned to one of over 120 bases around the United States. Starting in April 1944, 100 WASP a month went to Orlando, Florida, for Officer Candidate School. The training lasted three weeks. Jackie wanted the civilian pilots to become more aware of military regulations and property, especially since she expected them to someday become AAF officers.

"When I heard about Pearl Harbor, I was horrified. I wanted to do something in the war. That's why I learned to fly."

— WASP Dori Marland Martin

Although it was initially thought that WASP would simply ferry planes across the nation, graduates' duties expanded quickly.

Portrait of two new Women's Airforce Service Pilots during WWII

Some WASP trained as B-17 turret gunners. Others became flight instructors in basics and instruments. Often, women taught the new male recruits to fly. Other pilots delivered personnel, supplies, and weapons. They also served as "tow-target" pilots — a dangerous job. They attached large target sleeves behind their planes for gunners to practice shooting at from the ground.

"You flew a pattern, and the gunners were on the ground and shot at your target, which you were towing. It wasn't too safe. You'd come home with holes in the tail of the airplane."

— *WASP Ruth Weller Kunkle*

Curtiss A-25 *Shrike* flown by a WASP

OPERATIONS TOW TARGET

PLANE	MISSION	T.O.	ACTUAL T.O.	ALTITUDE	RA. STA.	FREQ.	OFF CO
8 016	Sears #4 TRK	1245		10,000	RRB-9	4130	1500
	Sears #6 TRK	1415		10,000	SC-41	4470	1630
8 805	Sears #4 TRK	1300		5,000	—	—	164
	Davis #5 TRK	1315		00	—	—	153
	Davis #1	11:45		0			15
	s #6			000		4470	14
44	rs #1	1515		0000		470	16
293	rs #3	1245		0		4470	15
	rs #1	16 15				470	17
7		1315				90	15
		10.30					
		1345				0	
		1345					
		1315				90	
		1615				2.90	
		1345					
		134					
		1230					

Pilots check their flight schedules.

In March 1944, Jackie starting sending WASP to
48 bases around the country specifically to fly broken
and repaired airplanes. These included planes with
issues documented by flight instructors or students.
Some men refused to fly these planes due to the risk
unless they were in combat.

Throughout their service, WASP piloted all 78 or
so types of airplanes flown during World War II. The
PT-17 Stearman was one of the first trainers. It was an
open-cockpit biplane for two. Avenger Field also had the
UC-78 Bamboo Bomber, which was a closed-cockpit
trainer. Two WASP eventually flew the B-29
Superfortress, America's newest bomber at the time.

Chapter 4

THE SACRIFICES WASP MADE

In the beginning, Jackie and Nancy believed that starting pilot organizations for women would happen faster if the pilots were civilians. The government would have taken too long to commission the women. In addition, civil service programs could be tested for success. If the program was successful, it was hoped that female pilots could be granted military status. This would give them recognition, consistency, and benefits.

As civilians, WASP didn't receive the same benefits as male cadets. They received $150 a month but had to pay for their housing, clothing, and food.

WASP pilot Bernice "Bee" Haydu in flight uniform

FACT

According to Jackie Cochran, WASP pilots flew upward of 60 million miles (97 million kilometers) in military aircraft between training and flying on assignment.

Male cadets only received $75 a month but didn't pay for their housing, clothing, or food. Male cadets also received insurance, medical and dental care, and $250 for a uniform upon graduation. WASP were issued partial uniforms worth $176.82. But they also had to spend $100 of their own money to complete the uniforms.

Despite similar training and expectations, WASP graduates received $250 a month, but had to pay for housing, clothing, and food, and any insurance they needed.

Trainees eating in the mess hall at Avenger Field

Perhaps the worst part of the WASP's civilian status was what happened when they were killed in service.

Families had to pay to get daughters home, and they couldn't receive survivor's benefits. The government didn't pay for civilian burials. Flags couldn't be draped on caskets as a military honor. WASP couldn't be buried at Arlington National Cemetery, a U.S. military cemetery.

In June 1944, Congress again denied the WASP militarization. America's allies in Europe were making progress against their enemies, and men were returning home. Both military and civilian pilots wanted their jobs back.

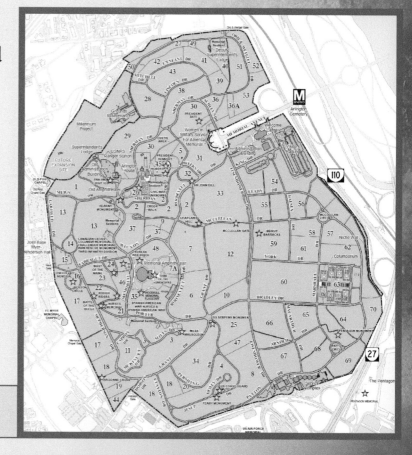

Arlington National Cemetery, Virginia

On June 26, 1944, General Arnold announced that Avenger would close. The last WASP class graduated on December 7, 1944, and the WASP went home on December 20, 1944.

Even after serving their country, the WASP did not receive veteran benefits, such as medical insurance, as male veterans did.

In fact, the pilots' records were marked classified and hidden from the public.

Burials for WASP Veterans

In 2002, a law was passed allowing WASP ashes to be buried at Arlington National Cemetery with full military honors. In March 2015, then–Secretary of the Army John McHugh repealed it. He believed the WASP didn't qualify.

The family of WASP Second Lieutenant Elaine Danforth Harmon, who died in April 2015, fought back to have her buried as a veteran. They started a petition, which gained nearly 180,000 signatures of support.

On May 20, 2016, President Barack Obama signed H.R. 4336 into law. It states the Department of Army must guarantee that the cremated remains of "persons whose service has been determined to be active duty service" may be placed in Arlington with full military honors. On September 7, 2016, Harmon was laid to rest at Arlington National Cemetery.

Chapter 5

GOLDEN WASP

Women flying military aircraft in an official capacity became a reality in the early 1970s. In 1974 Second Lieutenant Sally Woolfolk became the first to fly for the Army. The same year, Lieutenant Barbara Allen Rainey became the first woman pilot in the Navy. Women started pilot training in the Air Force in 1976. A year later, Janna Lambine became the first Coast Guard pilot. But the WASP knew they had been the first women to fly military missions.

Through letters to and meetings with politicians, the WASP finally received active duty recognition. President Jimmy Carter signed a law in 1977 that gave the women veteran status.

WASP, their daughters, military pilots, and lawmakers convinced Congress to pass a bill awarding the WASP the Congressional Gold Medal, the highest honor given to a civilian. President Barack Obama signed the bill on July 1, 2009. The WASP were finally recognized as both civilians and veterans and awarded for their brave service.

FACT

Fifinella, first the mascot of the WFTD and then of the WASP, was created by Walt Disney.

The National WASP WWII Museum is located at Avenger Field in Sweetwater, Texas. There are models of the airplanes, collectibles, and even handprints of some of the WASP.

"You and more than 900 of your sisters have shown that you can fly wingtip to wingtip with your brothers. If ever there was any doubt in anyone's mind that women can become skilled pilots, the WASP have dispelled that doubt . . . I salute you and all the WASP. We of the Army Air Force are proud of you; we will never forget our debt to you."

— General Henry "Hap" Arnold, farewell speech, December 20, 1944

TIMELINE

September 28, 1939

Jacqueline Cochran sends a letter to first lady Eleanor Roosevelt, saying that women pilots could help free up men to go overseas if the United States went to war.

September 10, 1942

The Women's Auxiliary Ferrying Squadron (WAFS) is established by Nancy Harkness Love.

November 16, 1942

The Women's Flying Training Detachment (WFTD) is established by Jacqueline Cochran.

August 5, 1943

The WAFS and WFTD merge into the Women Airforce Service Pilots (WASP).

December 7, 1944

The last WASP class graduates.

December 20, 1944

The WASP deactivates; the last WASP return home.

November 23, 1977

The WASP earn veteran status after President Jimmy Carter signs the bill, Public Law 95-202, Section 401, into law.

1984

The WASP receive World War II Victory Medals; those who served at least one year are awarded the American Theater Campaign Medal.

June 10, 2002

A law is passed allowing WASP to be interred at Arlington National Cemetery with full military honors.

July 1, 2009

The WASP are awarded the Congressional Gold Medal signed into law by President Barack Obama.

March 10, 2010

The Congressional Gold Medal ceremony is attended by over 250 surviving WASP.

March 23, 2015

Then-Secretary of the Army John McHugh repeals the law allowing WASP to be interred at Arlington.

May 20, 2016

President Barack Obama signs a law that states the Department of Army must guarantee that cremated remains of WASP can be placed in Arlington with full military honors.

Glossary

aeronautical [air-oh-NAHT-uh-kohl]—relating to the science of flight

bias [BYE-us]—prejudice

cadets [cuh-DEHTZ]—military school students

classified [KLAS-uh-fyd]—secret

commercial [cuh-MUR-shul]—having to do with money

commission [cuh-MISH-un]—the giving of military rank

ferry [FEH-ry]—to fly a plane from one place to another to deliver it

gender [JEHN-dur]—male or female

inter [in-TUHR]—to bury

personnel [PURS-un-ehl]—employees

petition [puh-TISH-un]—to ask for, often in writing, with many people

protocol [PROHT-uh-cahl]—customs and regulations

racial [RAY-shuhl]—having to do with race or ethnicity

turret [TUR-it]—a rotating structure on a plane, tank, or ship

Read More

Coleman, Miriam. *Women in the Military*. New York: Rosen Publishing Group, 2015.

Moss, Marissa. *Sky High: The True Story of Maggie Gee*. New York: Random House Children's Books, 2009.

Nathan, Amy. *Yankee Doodle Gals: Women Pilots of World War II*. Washington, D.C.: National Geographic Society, 2001 (updated).

Internet Sites

Use FactHound to find Internet sites related to this book.

Here's all you do:
Visit *www.facthound.com*

Just type in 9781515779377 and go.

Critical Thinking Questions

1. Jackie Cochran and Nancy Love both wanted to start a women's pilot organization. Why do you think they didn't work together sooner?

2. How did the WASP perform as compared to men pilots? Use evidence from the text to support your answer.

3. Look at Chapter 4. How has the tone of the book changed? What words and phrases help you determine this?

Index